SIMPLY**SCIENCE**

The Simple Science of
LIGHT

Emily James

a Capstone company — publishers for children

Raintree is an imprint of Capstone Global Library Limited, a company incorporated in England and Wales having its registered office at 264 Banbury Road, Oxford, OX2 7DY – Registered company number: 6695582

www.raintree.co.uk
myorders@raintree.co.uk

Edited by Jaclyn Jaycox
Designed by Jenny Bergstrom
Original illustrations © Capstone Global Library Limited 2018
Picture research by Jo Miller
Production by Tori Abraham
Originated by Capstone Global Library Limited
Printed and bound in China

ISBN 978 1 4747 4349 5
21 20 19 18 17
10 9 8 7 6 5 4 3 2 1

British Library Cataloguing in Publication Data
A full catalogue record for this book is available from the British Library.

Acknowledgements
We would like to thank the following for permission to reproduce photographs: Shutterstock: DVarela, back cover, Gelpi, 10-11, Horiyan, 29 (inset), Len Green, 20-21, Monkey Business Images, 27 (inset), moomsabuy, 11 (inset), nednapa, 22-23, Okhotnikova Ekaterina, 4-5, Perry Correll, 17, PointImages, 16, PongMoji, 28, rck_953, 18-19, Ronnachai Palas, 14-15, Ruslan Guzov, 7, Suzanna Tucker, 24-25, Suzanne Tucker, 8-9, Trong Nguyen, 26-27, WileeCole Phototgraphy, 29 (left), XiXinXing, 25 (inset), Yuganov Konstantin, 6, Zurijeta, 12-13. Design elements: Shutterstock: Macrovector, Skylines

CONTENTS

Delightful light. 4

Where does
    light come from?. 8

What makes shadows? 10

All about reflections 14

How are rainbows made? 20

Invisible colours. 24

How is light used? 26

Make a rainbow!. 28

Glossary. 30

Find out more 31

Comprehension
    questions 32

Index 32

Delightful light

Your shadow plays on a sunny day.
Water sparkles and shines. At a storm's
end, a rainbow bends.

Wherever you look, light dazzles and
dances. It makes wonderful shapes
and colours.

Light lets you see things. The brighter the light, the more you can see. Without light, you cannot see anything.

You see an object when light bounces off
it. Do you sometimes see shadows and
shapes in a dark room? If so, a bit of light
is sneaking in!

where does light come from?

Light comes from the sun. It is so bright
that we can even see on cloudy days.
Lightning, fireflies and the northern
lights also make natural light.

At night we may make our own light
to see. We may switch on light bulbs.
We may make a fire.

What makes shadows?

Light travels in rays. See the streams of
light shooting out of a film projector
in a dark cinema? See the beam shining
from a torch?

A spot of darkness forms when a
solid object blocks light rays. This spot
is called a shadow. Shadows fall behind the
object blocking the light.

11

Your body is a solid object. On a sunny day, it blocks sunlight's path and forms a shadow. The sun can shine *on* you, but it can't shine *through* you.

Walk towards the sun, and your shadow is behind you. Walk away from the sun, and your shadow is in front of you.

All about reflections

Everything you see reflects light, including trees, cars and people. Without reflected light, we can't see. Some objects reflect more light than others.

When light hits something smooth and shiny, most of the light rays bounce off it. Look in a mirror. Light rays are bouncing from you to the mirror and back again. Your image is a reflection.

Reflections aren't seen only in mirrors.
They appear all around your house!

Look at a shiny spoon or a silver toaster. Can you see yourself? Look at a black TV screen. Do these reflections look different from the one in the mirror?

The moon has no light of its own. It's lit
by the sun. Moonlight is light reflecting off
the moon.

At night, the reflection lights your path.
It paints the trees silver. It makes
buildings glow.

How are rainbows made?

A ray of sunlight is like a rope that's made of many strands. Each strand has its own colour: red, orange, yellow, green, blue or violet.

After a storm, water droplets fill the air. When sunlight shines through them, the rays bend. As they bend, all the colours in the rays separate. A rainbow forms!

You might even see a rainbow on a cloudless day. Look closely at a soap bubble. See the rainbow?

Find a rainbow in the spray of a garden hose. You can also see rainbow colours in a sparkling diamond.

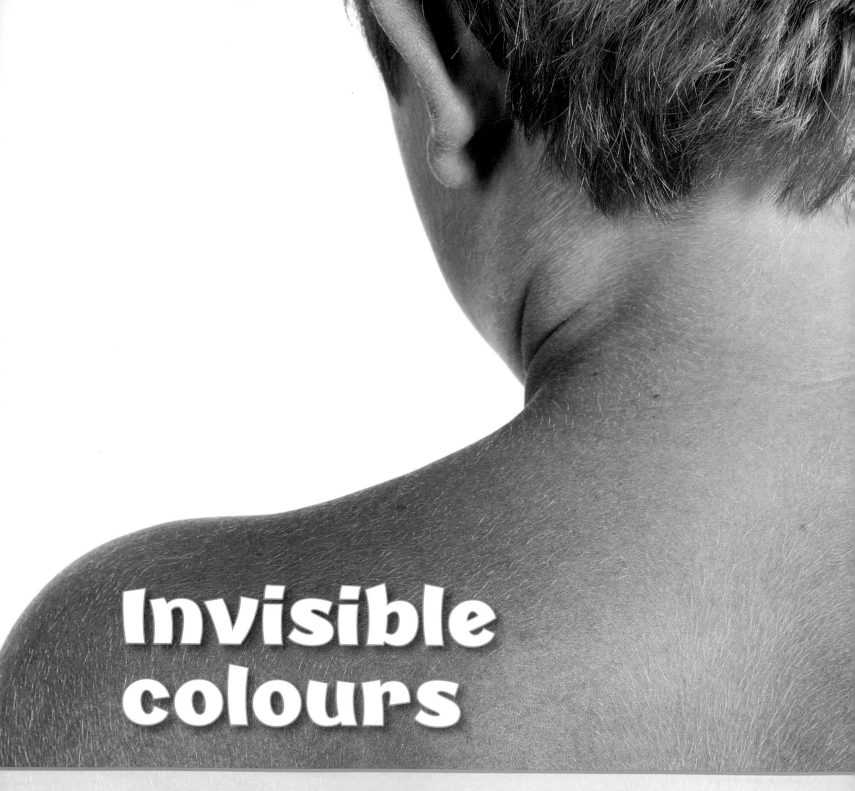

Invisible colours

There are some colours of the rainbow that people can't see. They are called infrared light and ultraviolet light. We feel infrared light as heat. Anything that gives off heat has infrared light.

The sun, a warm pavement and even your body all have infrared light. The sun also gives off a lot of ultraviolet light. This is the light that makes sunburns. Ouch!

How is light used?

Light is a big part of our lives. We need it to work and play. Without light, plants couldn't grow. Without plants, we wouldn't have any food to eat.

All around us, light is sparkling, swirling and blinking. It's bending and bouncing. Watch! Wonder! See all the colourful things to explore!

Make a rainbow!

Rainbows are amazing! They are full of colour and seem to appear out of nowhere. Try this fun activity to see if you can make your very own rainbow!

What you need:

a bowl a small mirror
water white paper

What you do:

- Fill a bowl with water and put it in a sunny spot.
- Place a mirror in the bowl, with its shiny side facing the sunlight. Be careful not to look at the sun in the mirror!
- Lean the mirror against one side of the bowl so it is standing up. (If it won't stand by itself, hold it with your hands.)
- Ask a friend to hold a piece of white paper outside the bowl, across from the mirror.
- What do you see on the white paper? How did it get there? Try tilting the mirror a bit. What happens?

GLOSSARY

beam ray or band of light from a torch, a car headlight or the sun

infrared light light that produces heat; humans cannot see infrared light

northern lights bright, colourful streaks of light that appear in the night sky in the far north

projector machine that shows films on a screen

reflect return light from an object

separate set, put or keep apart

shadow dark shape made when something blocks light

strand small, thin piece of something that looks like a string

ultraviolet light invisible form of light that can cause sunburns

FIND OUT MORE

BOOKS

All About Light (All About Science), Angela Royston
(Heinemann Raintree, 2016)

Light (How Does Science Work?), Carol Ballard
(Wayland, 2014)

Light (Moving Up With Science), Peter Riley
(Franklin Watts, 2016)

WEBSITES

www.bbc.co.uk/guides/zp23r82
Learn more about light on this website.

**www.childrensuniversity.manchester.ac.uk/
interactives/science/earthandbeyond/shadows**
Find out how shadows made by the sun change
through the day.

COMPREHENSION QUESTIONS

1. At night, we need to make our own light to see. Name three ways you can make light.
2. The moon has no light of its own. How does it light up at night?
3. The sun gives off ultraviolet light. What is it? Hint: Use the glossary for help!

INDEX

colours 5, 20, 21, 23, 24, 27

infrared light 24–25

light rays 10–11, 15, 20, 21

mirrors 15, 16, 17

natural light 8

rainbows 4, 21, 22–23, 24

reflections 14–15, 16–17, 18–19

shadows 4, 7, 11, 12–13

storms 4, 21

sunlight 8, 12–13, 20, 21

ultraviolet light 24–25